Manners for the modern DOG

By
Gwen Bohnenkamp

Published by
PERFECT PAWS Publishing
fax: 650-745-2647
website: www.perfectpaws.com

Library of Congress No. 2-786-055
ISBN 0-9644601-0-6

About The Author

Gwen Bohnenkamp is an internationally recognized author and behaviorist. As President of Perfect Paws, Inc. in San Francisco, Gwen provided training and consultation services to pet owners, veterinarians and humane associations throughout the United States and Canada. As Vice President of The Center for Applied Animal Behavior in Berkeley California, she co-authored a series of behavior booklets with veterinarian Dr. Ian Dunbar. At the San Francisco SPCA, Gwen founded and directed the largest and most comprehensive animal behavior correction program in the United States. She established and implemented the San Francisco SPCA's Animal Behavior Hotline, the country's first call-in animal behavior correction service.

During her career, Gwen has spoken on the topic of animal behavior for numerous local, civic and professional organizations, including the Commonwealth Club of California. Gwen has appeared in a variety of media including TV (where she had her own segment titled "Pet Calls"), newspaper and magazine (People Magazine, Ladies Home Journal, Better Homes and Gardens, TV Guide); and for over eight years appeared on Northern California's most popular news-talk radio station, answering questions on animal behavior. Gwen has instructed a course on Applied Animal Behavior at San Francisco State University and is the author of *Manners for the Modern Dog; Help! My Dog Has An Attitude; From the Cat's Point of View* and *Raising Kaylee.*

For
Omaha & Nikki

Special Thanks
to
My Husband John

Cover Design and Illustrations
by Robert Mesarchik

Layout and Design
by John Simon

Contents

Communicating
With Your Dog

"Earth to Rover, Do You Copy?"

The most important time in your dog's life is right now. Your dog's behavior is constantly changing. A dog that is well-behaved today will not necessarily remain that way forever. New problems can always develop. If your dog is not a Lassie-replica, existing problems can get worse.

Dogs are animals and without proper training, they will behave like animals. They will soil your house, destroy your belongings, bark excessively, dig, fight other dogs and even bite you. Nearly all behavior problems are perfectly normal, natural and necessary dog activities that occur at the wrong time or place or are directed at the wrong thing. For example, a dog will eliminate on the carpet instead of outside; bark all night long instead of just when a stranger is prowling around outside; or chew furniture or shoes instead of his own toys. The key to preventing or treating behavior problems is learning to teach your dog to redirect his normal behaviors to outlets that are acceptable in the domestic setting.

Puppyhood

Puppyhood is a crucial time in a dog's life. This is the time when experiences have a major effect on shaping the dog's future personality. One of the most important aspects of a dog's personality is how he interacts with other animals and people. Give your puppy plenty of opportunity to meet a variety of people during his impressionable, formative weeks. If he is expected to get along with other animals, make a point of introducing him to them while he is growing up. However, until your pup has received his full course of puppy shots, don't allow him on the streets, and only introduce him to healthy dogs that have perfect vaccination records; otherwise he could get one of the more serious canine diseases.

Socialization occurs naturally if puppies are allowed to play and interact freely with other dogs. Puppies that are raised with little or no contact with other dogs will often turn out to be asocial or even anti-social towards them. Some pups spend their early months isolated in kennels.

Many of these pups do not receive enough human contact during this sensitive period and may not be socialized towards people. Instead they grow up to be fearful or shy of people.

During early puppyhood, it is important for you to keep an eye open for any signs of shyness or fearfulness. A little socialization during puppyhood will go a long way to bolster the dog's confidence. Don't delay. With problems such as shyness, the older the dog, the greater the challenge. A dog that has not had the benefit of early socialization is not a lost cause. However, the amount of time, energy, and patience required to train him will be much greater.

The Second Hand Dog

When in a new, unfamiliar setting, a dog will often be on her best behavior. Why? Because she's assessing the situation. It's as if she is asking herself: What are the rules in this house? Who is top dog here? What am I allowed to chew? Where am I allowed to sleep? When do I have to obey these people and when can I get away with ignoring them?

Your dog will be especially sensitive and impressionable during the first few weeks in her new home. The early experiences in her new household will leave a permanent impression. As such, it is the best time to re-educate a dog that has inherited problems from a previous owner or unknown background. Any effort you make now will have a pronounced and long lasting effect that will set a precedent for years to come.

Since dogs tend to sum up new people and situations very quickly, it's important to provide guidelines as soon as possible. If your dog is allowed unsupervised, free access to the house and yard, she will assume that there are no restrictions on her behavior. If you do not provide some set of rules and regulations, then she will make up her own.

Guard against allowing your dog too much freedom too soon. Initially, keep her fairly calm and quiet. Then, over a period of a couple of weeks, gradually increase the number and length of on-leash walks and fun training sessions. Off-leash training and romps may begin immediately in your home and yard. As your dog demonstrates her reliability and confidence, you may progress to dog run areas. By gradually increasing her freedom over a couple of weeks, you are able to keep a close eye on the development of her behavior. Additionally, your dog can continue to savor her ever expanding freedom with the confidence that it is likely to last for a very long time. . . for a lifetime.

Learning by Experience

Whether you have a puppy, a newly adopted dog or dog that has been with you for many years, the most important time to prevent or solve problems is right now! The key to problem solving is communication. Since dogs don't speak or understand English and we don't speak Canine, then how can we effectively communicate with our pet?

Before we can communicate with our dogs, we must understand how they learn. Very simply, dogs learn by experience. If the experience is good, they will want to repeat the experience. If the experience is bad, they won't. Many dog trainers refer to this as a reward / reprimand system. If the dog behaves appropriately, reward her; if the dog behaves inappropriately, reprimand or correct her. If this is so simple, then why do we have so much trouble putting theory to practice? There are two reasons.

First, our interpretation of a reward or reprimand may be entirely different from the dog's interpretation. What we think is a reprimand, the dog may actually think is a reward. For example, when the dog jumps up excitedly to see us, we often push and shove her away. The dog may think this is a fun game and continue to jump up. If the dog is barking and we start yelling at her, she may think we're joining in on the barking, or actually encouraging her.

Many times we unintentionally reward or reprimand our dog. Without even knowing it, we are shaping our dog's behavior and teaching her bad habits. Dogs are always learning - whether we intend to teach them or not. For example, in a well meaning attempt to soothe your dog when she is frightened, you cuddle, stroke and baby talk to her. She thinks she's doing the right thing in acting fearful because you appear so approving of it. She doesn't understand that there's nothing to be afraid of, she just knows she's getting extra special attention and affection from you when she is acting fearful.

While sitting in a veterinarian's office, many people try to quiet their barking dog by giving her biscuits and stroking her behind the ears. No wonder the dog barks! I'd bark too if I could get special treats and a massage.

The second reason we have trouble putting into practice the "learning by experience" theory, is because the timing of our rewards and reprimands is faulty. Whatever the dog experiences at the exact moment of the activity determines whether she'll repeat it or not. It's a pleasant and rewarding experience for the dog to eat garbage out of the trash can, no matter what we say about it three hours later or even three seconds later.

If you're trying to teach your dog to sit and she does so upon your request, then 20 minutes later you reward her, you're not teaching her to sit on request or command. Timing is critical. If your dog sits, then immediately jumps up to snatch a biscuit from your hand, she is being rewarded for jumping up and grabbing the biscuit, not for sitting. With some dogs, this can happen in 3/10ths of a second. The reward must come right when the dog sits, so she knows what you are trying to teach her. The same principle applies when you're trying to teach your dog not to do something - the unpleasant experience (or the reprimand) must accompany the misbehavior. One special note here: never punish or reprimand your dog for peeing or pooping in the wrong place, even if you catch her in the act of going on your oriental carpet. Read the section on housetraining for details.

Whatever the dog is doing at the very instant she receives either the reward or reprimand, that is what she is learning to do or not to do. So if you come home and scold your dog when she runs to greet you, you are punishing her for saying hello even though you think you are scolding her for ripping up the mail or whatever. The only effective way to teach your dog not to misbehave is to catch her in the act of misbehaving. And the only way to prevent her from misbehaving when you are not there to correct her is to confine her to a place where she can do no damage.

He Knows He's Been Bad

We often assume our dog knows he's been bad because when we return home, we find him hiding, slinking around with his tail between his legs and looking very guilty. In dog language, what he is saying is "Oh no, I know you're angry, I know you're going to scold me, please don't beat me or yell at me." And what do we do? We yell at or spank our dog. Dogs know we're upset because they can detect even a fractional increase in our heart rate, breathing and body temperature. They can read our facial expressions and body language. All these things signal that we are angry.

It's rare that a dog showing obvious signs of submission will be further harassed by another dog. So when we continue to scold him after he has made his submissive or "I'm so sorry, I'm just a worthless worm" gesture, he becomes even more confused. In an effort to please us, he may even start to submissively urinate. If this has already happened, read the section on submissive urination. If the dog is pushed too far, he may become frightened and he may feel the need to defend himself by growling or snapping.

Dogs that are left alone for even a couple of hours anxiously await your return. On the one hand, they are happy you are coming home, but on the other hand, they are worried that you may be angry or aggressive when you do return. This creates a lot of psychological stress. When dogs are stressed, they often become hyperactive and vent their excess energy in doggy fashion by barking, chewing or digging. Stress can often stimulate their bowels and cause them to soil your house. More often than not, punishing a dog long after or even minutes after he has misbehaved leads to more and greater problems.

Reward

The single most important aspect of training is rewarding the dog for good behavior. The more times the dog is rewarded, the quicker she will learn. Therefore, it's essential that you set up situations repeatedly in order for the dog to get lots of practice at doing the right thing. It's equally as important that you always praise your dog for good behavior instead of taking it for granted. It's easy to forget to praise good behavior because it goes unnoticed. But the very nature of misbehavior gets our attention.

We don't notice when our dog is lying quietly but excessive barking gets our attention. When the dog does her business outside, we come to expect it and also ignore it. But if the dog has an accident inside, it's suddenly a big deal. How many of us take notice and praise our dogs when they chew their own toys? It's more natural for us to go berserk when we find our favorite pair of shoes chewed up!

Praise and reward are the most important part of

maintaining good behavior and preventing problems from arising. It is our responsibility to remember to reward and praise our dog frequently when she is being good. And being good may sometimes simply consist of just not being naughty at the moment.

Reprimand

Some dogs feel they are constantly bombarded with "No! Stop that! Bad dog! Get off!" They tend to get used to it so that the reprimands become meaningless and are ignored. If most of our interaction with our dog is praise for good behavior, then reprimands will take on much more meaning. Whenever you find the need to reprimand your dog, immediately show him what you want him to do, then reward him for getting it right. If you catch him chewing the furniture, shout "OFF!" Then immediately direct him to his own toys, enthusiastically entice him to chew on them and praise him for doing so.

If done correctly, your voice alone is sufficient for reprimand. A correct reprimand is short, sharp and immediate. It should instantly produce the desired result. If your dog ignores you, your reprimand is ineffective, so don't continue repeating what doesn't work. Instead, either increase the reprimand or change it to let him know without a doubt that you are displeased.

Don't continually nag your dog and never reprimand him unless you catch him in the act. If you come home and the trash is scattered around, don't get mad at your dog. Reprimand yourself or your roommate for leaving the trash out where your dog could get to it.

Obedience Training

Give Your Dog Some Class

Why?

One of the best things you can do for yourself and your dog is to obedience train him. Obedience training doesn't solve all behavior problems, but it is the foundation for solving just about any problem. Training opens up a line of communication between you and your dog. Effective communication is necessary to teach your dog what it is you want him to do. Once your dog starts learning, he acquires a learning ability. Then you can teach him: "stay" (don't bolt out the door); "sit" (don't jump up on the visitors); "off" (don't chew the furniture); or "quiet" (enough barking already!).

Training is also an easy way to establish the social hierarchy. When your dog obeys the simple request of "come here, sit" he is showing compliance and respect for you. It is NOT necessary to establish yourself as the top dog or leader of the pack by using extreme measures such as the so-called alpha roll-over. You CAN teach your dog his subordinate role by teaching him to show submission to you with a paw raise ("shake hands"), roll over or hand lick ("give me a kiss"). Most dogs love performing tricks (obedience commands) for you which also pleasantly acknowledge that you are the boss.

Training should be fun and rewarding for both you and the dog. It can enrich your relationship and make living together more enjoyable. A well-trained dog is more confident and can more safely be allowed greater freedom than an untrained dog.

When?

Some people debate whether or not it is possible to train puppies, while others ask if it is possible to teach an old dog new tricks. The answer to both questions is a definite YES. Whatever the age of your dog, the right time to begin training is NOW!

Where?

Enroll in a local dog training class to learn the basics. Then most training can, and should be done in your own home. It is best to start teaching your dog in a familiar area with as few distractions as possible. Once your dog has a clear understanding of what you want him to do, then it's important that you practice in all places you expect to have control over him.

Practice in every room in your house, in your yard, in your car, in your friend's house, at the park, at the beach; practice everywhere and anywhere you and your dog go together.

How?

With some dogs, an extreme amount of affectionate given at the wrong time can often do more harm than good. Many dogs receive buckets of praise and affection just for lazily laying their head on their owner's lap. Repeated large doses of free affection will reduce its effectiveness as a reward. If your dog can get all the affection he wants for just breathing, why on earth should he "sit" for an ounce of praise? Other dogs thrive on attention and affection and there is no such thing as too much. You will know by your dog's responsiveness.

Once your dog has mastered the basics, it's important to keep practicing or your dog will forget his training. Instead of having long, boring practice sessions, it is better to practice for 10 seconds at a time throughout the day. In other words, training should be integrated into your daily routine. Keep training both enjoyable and meaningful.

The best way to integrate training is to ask your dog to

perform quick and simple commands before all enjoyable activities. For example, before taking your dog for a walk, ask him to sit-stay while you put on his collar and leash. Next, he has to lie down before going through the door. Your dog will quickly learn that if he obeys, he gets to go for his walk. If he doesn't obey, the outing is delayed until he does. Ask your dog to "come, sit, down-stay" before giving him his dinner. If your dog likes to fetch, ask him to sit or lie down each time he wants you to throw the ball for him. If he obeys, the game continues, if he doesn't obey, the game is over. Training should always be a part of your dog's favorite activities and daily routine.

Jumping Up

Dogs jump up because they want to say hello, and we humans usually say hello back by praising, petting and rewarding them when they do jump up. Often we think it's cute and fun when they're puppies or when we first get them as pets because we want to show them how much we love them. It's hard to resist a cuddly puppy when he's being cute and affectionate. But as the puppy grows or the novelty of a new pet wears off, the jumping up becomes obnoxious and tiresome. So begin right away by not allowing or rewarding this behavior. Shouting at your dog may excite him even further, causing him to jump up even more. Reprimanding in a sweet voice or gently pushing your dog away can be another reward for jumping up.

When your dog jumps up on you, do NOT kick, knee, or step on his feet. These antiquated methods are inhumane, dangerous and generally do not work. Teach your dog that there are alternative ways to say hello and receive attention.

The best thing to do is to teach your dog to sit. When he's sitting, then kneel down and give him a big hug and kiss. Your dog can't sit and jump up at the same time. Practice the training sessions over and over; whenever visitors arrive at the front door; when meeting people on walks; and even when you return home. It will be difficult at first, but with every repetition, it will get easier and easier, so be patient and keep trying.

Instead of practicing once or twice a day, practice 20 times in one afternoon. Leave the house through the back door and return immediately through the front door. As you come in, ask your dog to sit. Stick with it until he sits, then reward and praise him lavishly. Leave again and return. Keep repeating this until your dog learns what to do and gets lots of practice and opportunities to get it right. Even the most excitable dogs eventually get so tired and bored with your coming and going, that they actually calm down and pay attention enough to sit either automatically or on the first request. This requires patience and repetition on your part, but the payoff is well worthwhile.

Pulling On Leash

This problem is most easily corrected before taking your dog out for a walk. In fact, the problem usually begins the moment you mention the word "walk." So this is where you first address the problem of pulling on leash. Begin by requiring your dog to calm down and sit-stay while you put the collar and leash on her. When she learns this stage, then proceed to the next step.

If she sits nicely while you put on her leash, but then begins to drag you out the door, then this is where you need to address the problem. If the walk begins out of control it most likely will remain out of control.

It's difficult to begin the training during a walk because of the many distractions - cars, people, sounds, and smells are all exciting and interesting to your dog. In this situation, your dog will get away with pulling much of the time, and therefore he will try his best to get away with pulling all of the time. No matter how much your dog strains, coughs and gags while pulling, he does it because he loves it, and each step he is allowed to take only reinforces the pulling behavior.

Put your dog on leash; but instead of going anywhere, stand still. Thinking that he is about to go for a walk, your dog will probably go bonkers, pulling, bouncing and dancing at the end of the leash. After five or ten minutes, he should calm down. Bring a book to read or your MP3 to listen to so that you have the patience to wait for however long it takes. Each time your dog stands still and does not strain on the leash, lavish him with praise. This will teach him that not-pulling is rewarded.

With this positive foundation, it is now time to teach him that pulling is not acceptable. Each time he pulls, softly say, "No pulling." The words "no pulling" are a request to stop pulling and also a warning that he will be reprimanded if he does not stop pulling. After giving the warning, one of two things must happen immediately. Either you will shower your dog with praise for not pulling or you will give a strong verbal reprimand "NO PULLING!" if he ignores your request.

After several repetitions, your dog will learn that he can avoid the correction by responding to your warning. If your dog is especially difficult, the entire family may need to join in the training. Once you warn him, the entire family can verbally reprimand him in unison if he should try pulling again. Many "tough" dogs respond well to group reprimands.

Once your dog will stand still on-leash while you are standing still, take a couple of steps towards the door. This will excite him again and you can repeat the exercise. After another series of repetitions, you will be ready to try to get out the front door with your dog. Do not let him forge ahead of you. If he tries to pull, verbally scold him, then walk away from the door and go sit down telling him that you're not going for a walk after all. He will soon learn that he doesn't even get to go through the door unless he is behaving nicely instead of dragging you along.

Having mastered a graceful exit from the house, it's now time to work on your dog not pulling while on his walk. First try standing still on the sidewalk in front of your home. Once your dog is under control, begin the walk. Each time he pulls or begins to forge ahead, give the warning "no pulling." If he stops pulling, praise him and continue the walk. If your dog dares to pull, shout "NO PULLING!" Immediately do a rapid about-turn and head off in another direction.

If he starts again to lunge ahead, keep repeating the about-turn. You can lure his attention away from the distraction that is causing him to pull by presenting a treat or toy to get his attention. Then have him sit-stay just so you can once again be in control of the situation. This sounds like a tedious process but it works. It's gentle and effective.

If the above method does not work, there are some tools (like the Gentle Leader and Halti and various training collars, etc) available which work wonderfully. It's best to have a professional trainer show you how to use these items without harming your dog. Using excessive force with these tools has been shown to cause cervical vertebrae subluxation and even permanent damage. Constant lunging on the part of your dog and constant yanking or pulling on your part can seriously damage your dog's neck and throat. Please do not allow this to happen. If used properly, the training tools are much gentler on you and your dog.

Barking
Sounds of Silence

Barking is a perfectly normal and natural canine behavior. But excessive barking at inappropriate times is an annoying problem. Dogs that are socially isolated or confined for long periods of time look for an activity to pass the time of day. A dog that is left alone all day might take up barking as a hobby because no one is there to control it. In no time at all, barking becomes an enjoyable habit and daily routine.

Some dogs are stressed, nervous and lonely when left alone and bark as a means of coping and venting their nervous energy.

Another reason your dog may bark is because you have trained her to bark. Poochie speaks and you obey. "Woof" and you open the door to let her out; "woof" and you open it again to let her in; "woof" and it's a treat; "woof" and it's a massage. The dog has learned to get attention by vocal blackmail.

Holistic Approach

The first step to solving a barking problem is to realize that the majority of dogs bark because they are lonely, bored, frustrated or frightened. These are all things that you can help alleviate. A well-exercised, happy dog will contentedly sleep the day away. Play with your dog to vent her energy. Get on the floor and have fun with your dog; spend time with her.

Many owners are told to take their dog on a 5 mile jog or hike to vent her energy so she will sleep all day. Yes, and so will the owner. Obviously this is not often useful or practical advice for those who are away from home 8 to 10 hours a day or who are not marathon athletes. But you can exercise and entertain your dog in a variety of other ways.

Have an indoor game of fetch. Set up a baby gate in a doorway between two rooms. Sit in one room and toss a ball or toy over the gate into the next room. The running and jumping will give your dog a good workout in a short period of time.

Another fun game is Hide & Seek. Put your dog in a sit-stay in one room and find a hiding place in another room. Your dog will eagerly search for you when you shout out the release command. Reward her with a big hug and a treat when she finds you. Dogs love this game and are willing to play even when you pick the most absurd hiding places.

Try doing some training indoors or in your backyard. A few dozen sit-stand-down sequences will be the equivalent of 50 human sit-ups or push-ups. But make it fun and rewarding or your dog will quickly get bored.

Dogs are social animals. They need friends and companionship. Take your dog to the same park daily or weekly and let her visit and make doggy friends. Dogs romping around and playing together tire rapidly and will sleep happily while recovering from a good, hardy play session.

If your dog really loves to bark, then set aside a time and place where neighbors won't be disturbed and say, "OK doggie, you want to bark? Then let's bark! Woof, woof, speak, speak!" It's easy to incite a barker to bark. Just get her excited and start a barking contest. See who can bark loudest and longest. After about 20 minutes of non-stop barking, your dog should not feel like barking again for days.

Barking is often caused by fear or uncertainty of noises and movements coming from outside. You can help alleviate some of the dog's anxiety by taking her for walks around the neighborhood. Let her investigate the mysterious sounds she hears when inside. Just knowing what causes these noises will often lessen her anxiety about them and your dog will no longer feel the need to bark nervously at them. You can also leave a radio or the TV on when you are away to help mask noises. My dogs seem to enjoy Animal Planet so I always leave that on when I go out.

Reward

Many of us are eager to reprimand our dog for barking, but we forget to praise her when she is quiet. It's easy to fall into this trap because the very nature of barking gets our attention. It's easy to forget to praise and reward our dog for being quiet because it's not as noticeable as when she is barking. Remember to praise your dog whether she is having a quiet moment on her own initiative, or whether she was instructed to "Be quiet."

There will be times when you want your dog to bark, for example, when a stranger comes to your front door. The domestic dog is one of the most sophisticated (certainly the most loveable) all purpose intruder alert/deterrent alarm systems. However, you should not take these functions for granted. Don't rely on the dog's territorial instinct to guard your house and property. Left to their own devices, most dogs will end up barking too much or too little.

The dog's natural inclination to sound the alarm has to be modified so that it fits your specific needs. Instead of haphazardly punishing your dog for barking one moment, yet ignoring her the next, you should make sure that you always praise your dog for sounding an appropriate alarm. Investigate what the dog has alerted you to. Thank her for doing a good job, then tell her that the job is over and to go lie down and be quiet.

"Quiet!"

Just as a dog can learn the meaning of the word "sit" and obey on command, so she can learn the meaning of the word "quiet" and obey on command. Each time the dog barks, after several woofs, she should first be praised for sounding the alarm and then softly asked to be quiet. If she remains quiet, she should be praised, but if she barks again, she should be immediately and effectively reprimanded. Start out by requiring your dog to be quiet for only a few seconds. As training progresses, the required period of silence should be increased.

Most dogs when barking will suddenly become quiet

when you wave a favorite treat in front of their face. When you have the dogs attention, say "Quiet.... good girl...... quiet." Then reward her silence with the treat. For the next treat she has to remain silent for 5 seconds, and then the next treat will require her to be silent for 7 seconds, and so on.

Within a single session it is possible to train your dog to stop barking and to be quiet for one to two minutes. At this stage, the barking problem is now well under control. After your dog has been quiet for a minute or so, whatever stimulus excited her to bark in the first place will most likely be gone.

So what do you do when the dog does not keep quiet for the requisite amount of time or doesn't stop barking at all after you've asked her to "Be quiet?" Since the dog has already learned that being quiet earns a reward, it's now time to show her what happens if she isn't quiet.

The instant your unsuspecting pooch ignores your request, her very next woof should be met with a cataclysmic, earth-rending, 120 decibel "BE QUIET!" She will most certainly cease barking. Most dogs are so totally shocked and amazed by this horrendous outburst that they stare at you in disbelief and silence. Praise and reward her as soon as she is quiet.

If however, she resumes barking before the requisite time is up, she should be immediately reprimanded again, but this time much more convincingly. Once the dog stops barking, immediately praise her and start counting out the seconds. Once she succeeds at 3 seconds, increase the quiet time to 5 seconds and so on.

The Big Secret

Most attempts at teaching a dog to 'be quiet' fail because of inconsistency. Sometimes the dog is punished for barking, sometimes she is ignored, and occasionally she is even praised for barking! The dog never clearly learns when it's OK to bark and when it is not.

The great secret to success in curing a barking problem is to never reprimand the dog for barking. Instead, reprimand the dog for disobedience - disobedience to your request for her to be quiet.

Once you have asked your dog to be quiet, one of two things must happen instantly. Either your dog obeys and is rewarded or your dog disobeys and is reprimanded.

More on Reprimands

The object of the reprimand is to get your dog to be quiet instantly. If the reprimand does not work, it is pointless to repeat it. There are many ways to convincingly reprimand a dog. If one method doesn't work with your dog, try another.

Every dog is unique and will respond differently to various methods. Try shouting and screaming, banging on the walls, rattling the furniture, dropping piles of magazines or trays of empty aluminum cans or stamping your feet. You must get the message across that you do not approve of disobedient barks.

As soon as your dog is quiet, instantly revert to your original sweet, charming self and calmly praise her.

For those of you who are not theatrically inclined, a squirt bottle is ideal. Fill the bottle with plain water and adjust the setting to 'jet stream' not 'misty spray.' When your dog disobediently barks, sternly say "QUIET!" and at the same time squirt her! After a few repetitions of the woof-squirt sequence, she will get the message. Don't forget to praise her after the squirt if she stops barking.

Some dogs think loud shouts and commotion are all part of a game, and they become very excited and bark even more. In this case, you may find that a reprimand in your lowest, most ice cold, I-mean-business tone of voice gets the message across more clearly.

Digging

The Hole Story

Dogs dig for many reasons: they dig to bury and recover bones; they dig cooling pits when it's hot and warming pits when it's cold; they dig up prey; and they dig dens. Dogs also dig because it's a highly enjoyable and normal canine activity. Lack of exercise, prolonged confinement, boredom and loneliness are general causes for behavior problems such as destructive digging.

If you provide your dog with plenty of opportunity for walks, runs, play and training, she probably won't develop a digging problem. But until your dog has been taught not to dig up your garden, she should not be given free access to the garden when you are not there to supervise her.

Reward

If your dog loves to dig, provide him with his own digging pit just as parents would provide their child with a sand box. Take your dog's needs into consideration when choosing a location for the pit. Don't have it directly in the blazing sun during the summer or unprotected against the cold wind of winter. A 3 by 6 foot area, about 2 feet deep is sufficient for any size dog. Dig it up to loosen the earth and remove any dangerous, buried objects. Mix in a little sand to help it drain in the rainy season. Let your dog watch the preparations and if he joins in to help, lavish him with praise.

Once the pit is ready, it's easy to get your dog to dig in it. Take some of his favorite treats and toys and let him watch you make a fuss over burying them. Call your dog over and help him dig things up. It may be necessary to leave a little part of the treat sticking up so he knows it's there. Once he gets the idea of scratching at the dirt to remove the treat or toy, you can start to bury them deeper and deeper.

All the time your dog is digging, enthusiastically repeat, "Dig in your pit, dig in your pit," and profusely praise him. When he finally discovers the treat, he is immediately rewarded by getting to eat it. If it's a ball or toy you've buried, then you can immediately play a short game of fetch, then bury it again. Repeat this over and over, always repeating the command, "Dig in your pit."

Your dog will quickly learn what the command means. You can test this by putting him inside the house or garage, burying a dozen or so treats and toys, and then letting him out. Say "Dig in your pit," and praise him if he goes to the pit. This training process can usually be done in one afternoon.

Once your dog has learned to dig in his pit, you must still verbally encourage and praise him whenever he shows any interest in the pit, and especially if he digs there without any verbal encouragement. Now, every morning before you leave for work, you can hide all kinds of things in the pit, which will keep your dog busy for hours. Even if he has found all the goodies, he will keep digging and looking to see if anything else is there.

Reprimand

Once your dog understands digging in his pit is an acceptable activity, and thoroughly understands the meaning of the command "Dig in your pit," you must now teach him that digging elsewhere is wrong.

The first step is to teach your dog to stay completely off the flower or vegetable gardens and that he is only allowed on other parts of the yard. Clearly demarcate the forbidden areas with a short fence about a foot high. A few small sticks with a length of string attached along the top is sufficient. The fence is not intended as a physical barrier but as a means of marking a boundary.

Spend the day outside and do some gardening or work on a suntan, but watch your dog closely. Each time he gets close to the boundary, quietly warn him by saying "Off." If one paw goes over the line, shout "OFF! OFF! OFF!" and charge at him. Continue shouting until all four paws are firmly on the correct side of the boundary and then immediately praise him.

If you invest a little time, your dog will quickly learn to keep out of the garden. As in the prior chapter in the section on reprimand for inappropriate barking, if your dog does not respond to your raised voice, you can try a squirt bottle with water or some other suggestions. Remember that group reprimands are also very effective, so you can enlist the help of your family.

To teach your dog not to dig anywhere but in his pit, it's time to set a trap. Put one or two drops of chicken broth or bacon drippings on the lawn. Again, spend the day outside and watch your dog closely. Eventually he will discover these spots and start to investigate. If he makes one scratch at the ground, immediately scream, "OFF! Dig in your pit, dig in your pit!"

This is an instructive reprimand: the loud "OFF" tells him he is making a mistake, and the instruction tells him what he should be doing. Run to the digging pit and entice your dog to dig as before and praise him as soon as he does so.

Repeat this procedure, but this time leave him in the yard by himself so he thinks he's alone and watch him from a window or around a corner. When he starts to dig and you come bursting out of nowhere, he will be further surprised as he thought he was not being supervised.

To discourage your dog from returning to a favorite digging spot, try burying inflated balloons, large rocks, shake cans, or a metal garbage can lid in the hole. These unpleasant surfaces should discourage your dog from digging there again. There are products and devices (such as the Invisible Fence) that can also be used to boundary train your dog. These work well for many dogs in keeping them out of designated areas, especially gardens, but I have seen them fail miserably when used to confine a dog within an area or property. There is a big difference between using these devices to keep dogs out of certain areas and keeping dogs in a certain area.

Aggression

Soothing the Savage Beast

THE PROBLEM

Aggression is the single biggest problem owners have with their dogs. Biting dogs often lead lives of isolation and confinement; the majority are euthanized. This is tragic because aggression can be prevented. Don't wait until your dog snaps at you or another person until you do something about it.

As dog owners, it is our responsibility to train and teach our dogs the rules of our society. If we don't want them to bite, then we should teach them not to bite. Biting is certainly normal and acceptable in canine society, but not in ours.

Contrary to popular belief, the big stick philosophy is usually unnecessary for the prevention and treatment of aggression. In most cases, countering force with force only makes the problem worse. It is possible to teach your dog to inhibit his biting behavior with the almost exclusive use of praise and reward.

THE CAUSE

Dogs bite because they are dogs, and this is one of the things that dogs do. They bite, just as they chew, dig, bark and wag their tail. It's normal dog behavior. Professional and academic textbooks will often list over 21 reasons why dogs bite. For our purposes, there are only three significant reasons your dog will bite.

Dominance

Dogs are pack animals and their social structure demands a leader - the alpha or top dog, as the position is often called. A top dog or leader is not an aggressive bully. Being the top dog means having special rights and privileges that come with the rank.

A top dog controls everything - possessions, resources, location, activity. Top dogs are usually kind, loving and benevolent. They are affectionate; they give and they share. But they are still the boss. They control the other pack members with a simple glance, a stare, a growl, a showing of teeth, or body posture. They don't rule by force or violence. They don't attack, fight or bite pack members unless challenged or if the subordinate doesn't comply.

So if your dog thinks he's top dog, this will explain why he appears schizophrenic. One minute he's craving affection and attention and the next second, he's growling and snapping. He's just trying to keep you in line and maintain control when you don't respect his more subtle forms of communication. When you challenge a top dog, he may bite you to remind you that he is top dog.

We often give our dog subtle and even blatant messages that he is indeed top dog. It may be something as simple as the dog nudging you to be petted. He is demanding your attention and you show obedience every time you give in and pet him. The dog speaks and you obey. Every time the dog goes to the door and speaks to be let outside or speaks to be let back inside, the dog is in essence demanding that you be his servant. The dog is saying, "Let me in!" or "Let me out!"

Leaving food out all day for your dog to nibble on whenever he wants, reinforces in his mind that he has control over the resources. This is a top dog privilege.

Every time the dog snaps at you and you withdraw because you don't want to get bitten; the dog has said, "Stop that!" and you have obeyed.

We often tend to overemphasize the bully part of the top dog. For the most part, the top dog is a nice guy. We only tend to notice the bad things because that's what gets our attention. We don't say to ourselves, "Oh boy, Rover sure is nice today allowing me to pet him." But we do take great notice when he bites us.

Top dog can take two forms. It can be the spoiled dog who demands his way and usually gets it. If he doesn't, then he growls and bites. The other top dog is the bully who outright pushes everyone around and it works because everyone is so afraid of him. We don't see a lot of bully-type dominant dogs because most owners won't accept living with a dog that they are frightened to death of. The spoiled top dog is very dangerous because we usually don't recognize it as a dominance problem.

Fun and Play

This form of biting is also extremely dangerous because we ignore it, excuse it, and forgive it. We say things like, "The dog didn't mean it," or "He was just playing." But these bites still hurt and can cause serious injury.

Insecurity

The majority of dog bites occur in this category. The dog feels he must protect or defend himself, his property or his territory. Someone invades his personal space; approaches him; reaches down to pet him; stands over him; touches one of his sensitive spots; or merely looks at him. All of these actions can be threatening to a dog. Dogs will often bite as a way of telling you that they are frightened or that they don't like what you are doing to them. It's their way of saying, "Quit it!" or "Stay away!" Many things that humans do are threatening to dogs, and the only way they know of coping is through aggression.

THE SOLUTION

There is no single solution for every case of aggression. Each dog is an individual and needs to be treated as such. You and your dog are a unique team and should have the counsel of an experienced and reputable animal behaviorist and trainer. However, any program for the treatment or prevention of aggression should include the following five points.

Leadership

Once a leader doesn't mean always a leader. If your dog considers himself top dog, you can change that. If you are currently seen as the leader, it's important that you maintain it. Remember that pack leaders are gentle, affectionate and loving. They don't rule by violence. Here is a simple, subtle and effective way for you to establish yourself as the top dog.

<u>NOTHING FOR FREE:</u>   Your dog must see you as the leader and provider of everything - food, water, toys, games, exercise, attention, comfort. Your dog must never be allowed to take or demand anything. You can give your dog absolutely anything he wants but only if he says "please" first. By all means, love and indulge your dogs. The difference is in how the goods and favors are dispensed. It'll be more fun spoiling your dog if you know he appreciates it and doesn't demand it or take it for granted. It's much better that the dog say, "Thank you, I love it when you spoil me," rather than "Give me that or I'll bite you."

So how do we get our dog to say please and thank you? By obeying a simple obedience command. Therefore, part of establishing yourself as leader is to OBEDIENCE TRAIN your dog so he knows how to sit, lie down or stay when you ask him to. Nothing is free for your dog anymore. There's no more nudging, pawing, barking to make you obey. In fact, the dog shows respect for you by obeying a simple obedience command before receiving anything. The dog must earn everything. This will establish you as top dog and in no way makes you a bully!

I would begin by completely hand feeding your dog all of his meals (provided the dog will take food from your hands without growling or biting you, if not, call a behaviorist immediately). Your dog must come and sit for every handful of dinner. If he doesn't obey - no dinner. Even if your dog doesn't know any obedience commands yet, you can still have him come to you for hand feeding.

Do this until you've enrolled him in a basic obedience course. For now, your dog is learning that you are the provider. You're the one who is in control of the food. You are the one who is dispensing it. Don't free feed your dog. Handing his food out and making your dog show obedience and compliance by doing a simple "sit" is a very strong statement that you are the leader.

CONSISTENCY: The second part of establishing yourself as top dog is: Your dog must obey. When you ask your dog to do something, don't let him learn that he can ignore or disobey you. Once you've asked your dog to do something, life does not go on until he does it. Don't confuse your dog by sometimes allowing disobedience and at other times disciplining him for the same thing. You must be consistent.

PUNISHMENT: The third part of establishing yourself as top dog is to NEVER use delayed punishment. Delayed punishment means punishing your dog for something he did hours, minutes or even seconds ago. Dogs do not understand this. In the canine world, top dogs are not unreasonable or unpredictable.

If you use delayed punishment, your dog will think you are untrustworthy. If your dog has misbehaved and you don't see him doing it, you should not punish him. Reprimand must accompany the crime. If you come home to a shredded couch, read the section on chewing - don't punish your dog.

Notice that we haven't yelled at the dog or used punishment or violence while establishing ourselves as top dog. The previous exercises are easy and can be performed with just about any dog.

The following exercises are usually safe to do with young puppies and dogs that have no history of aggression as preventive measures. With other dogs, you should work closely with a trainer or behaviorist while performing these exercises. You know your own dog and how far you can push him.

The most important point is that you progress very slowly and gently and prevent the dog from growling or biting for 2 reasons. First, we don't want you or anyone else to be bitten. Second, we don't want the dog to bite because every time he does, the behavior is reinforced. Every time the dog bites and gets away with it, the harder it is to cure the problem.

Bite Inhibition

Much of a puppy's early life is spent roughhousing and play-fighting with his litter mates. Typically, the pups roll around trying to bite each other's legs, ears, tail and scruff. Eventually, one puppy bites another too hard and the one that was bitten lets out a sharp, high-pitched yelp. The biter is usually startled by the sudden, loud noise, and the play session momentarily ends.

After a while, the puppy learns that it is his own overly rambunctious and aggressive behavior that causes the frightening noise and the end of a fun game. This is how dogs learn to play and bite each other gently. Using this same method, we can teach our puppy that biting humans is wrong. Take time to play-fight and gently roughhouse with your puppy. Do not be overly rough and do not do anything to frighten or hurt the puppy.

However, each and every time he bites, let out a loud, high-pitched screech, then walk away and ignore him for a few minutes. Again, your puppy will learn that it is his own overly aggressive behavior that leads to the reprimand. Do not hit your puppy to reprimand him. The scream and abrupt end of the play session are enough punishment.

Another way to teach and remind your dog to be gentle with his teeth is to offer a food treat and softly ask him to "Take it gently." If he tries to take it gently, then give lots of praise and let your dog have his treat. If he tries to snap it away or nips your fingers, or if his teeth even touch your fingers in the process, then act as if you've been hurt and don't let him have the treat until he is more gentle. When your dog's teeth touch your fingers, usually a short, sharp, high-pitched OUCH will do the trick. Most dogs don't want to hurt you; it's just that they don't know they are hurting you unless you tell them in a way they can understand.

Confidence Building

When it comes to confidence building, or helping your dog overcome his insecurities, your only option is to teach your dog through experience. Your dog will not learn by what you tell him verbally. You must show and prove to your dog over and over again and convince him through experience that certain things are not threatening and there is no need to feel insecure, defensive or aggressive.

The ultimate goal is to have your dog look forward to and welcome events and things that in the past caused him to feel defensive, protective or upset.

Dogs don't naturally like being held, squeezed or grabbed. They need to learn not to squirm and bite when being groomed, examined by a veterinarian or just touched and petted by overly affectionate people, especially children. Following are a variety of exercises as examples of how to proceed.

While performing these or any other handling exercise, if your dog objects or acts frightened, slow down and proceed more slowly. It is better to go too slowly and succeed than to go too quickly and fail. Every time the experience is unpleasant for your dog, it will take longer to convince him that there's no reason to be upset.

<u>EARS:</u> It is important to be gentle and patient while gradually building your dog's confidence to accept and

enjoy an ear exam. First, playfully scratch him behind the ears, praising him profusely and even offering a treat. Then try to gently hold his ear for just a second. If he does not object, again praise him profusely and reward him with a treat. Then try holding his ear for two seconds, three seconds and so on before he is given a treat.

Your dog should soon get the idea that having his ears handled is a good thing. Then try to fold back his ear and look inside, all the time praising him for good behavior and rewarding with an occasional food treat. At this stage, it should be possible to gently wipe the inside of the ear with a moist piece of gauze.

MOUTH: When examining your dog's mouth, first gently slide a thumb under the upper lip to expose his teeth from the outside. Using the same method described above for handling his ears, teach him to accept having his mouth opened and looked into. Go slowly until it is possible to hold open his mouth and examine his teeth. Again, praise your dog profusely and periodically reward him with a treat or two.

Work slowly, day by day, and always be sensitive to your dog's disposition. Once he is confident about having his mouth handled, it should be possible to try to clean his teeth, one tooth a day. Be sure to use liver flavored toothpaste made especially for dogs.

<u>PAWS:</u> Start out by giving a pleasant and enjoyable massage at your dog's shoulder and work down to his paws. Gently hold his paw for only a second and then let go. Increase the time that his paws can be held. Training your dog to shake hands often helps because it makes a game out of the exercise. Gently spread his toes and feel the spaces in between.

Then introduce your dog to the nail clippers: just touch each paw with the clippers and reward him with a treat. The next day, try to partially trim just one nail and then praise him if he does not object. Try another nail the next day and so on. Your veterinarian or groomer can give you some pointers on how to properly trim your dog's nails. And even if you don't plan to trim his nails yourself, go ahead and do these exercises anyway so that when the groomer trims his nails, it isn't a fearful or traumatic experience for him.

HAND SHYNESS: In the beginning, encourage your dog to approach to take a treat from your hand. Begin to accustom him to being reached for and touched. Repeatedly reach down to pet your dog with one hand and each time give him a treat with the other hand. Praise your dog all the time. At first reach down very slowly and pet your dog gently.

As the exercise proceeds, you may reach down quicker and pet him more vigorously. The aim is for the dog to associate a rapidly approaching hand with lots of praise and a plentiful supply of treats.

RESTRAINT: Restraint is not much different from a hug. When restraining your dog, at first, hold him gently and loosely and only for a short period. Praise him all the time he remains calm. If he struggles, then you are trying to do things too quickly. Once he is accustomed to close physical restraint, you may pick him up and hold him for just a couple of seconds, praising him all the time that he remains calm. From day to day, gradually increase the length of time that he may be held.

EYE CONTACT: In dog language, a stare is threatening, so we must slowly and gently teach our dog that a stare from a human is not a threat. To accustom your dog to being stared at, glance into his eyes for an instant and immediately praise and reward him. Once he gets used to you looking into his eyes for an instant, your glances can become looks and finally stares. Speaking softly will often encourage your dog to look at you. Occasionally give him a treat and soon he will learn that being stared at is no threat.

POSSESSIONS: It is natural for dogs to feel protective and possessive of property. We lock the doors to our homes and install alarms in our cars to keep intruders out and to keep our belongings safe. Dogs are no different, however the only way they have to protect what they think is their property is through aggression. Therefore, it is important to convince your dog that there will always be enough toys, food or bones to go around and therefore no need to try to protect them.

Your dog must also learn that all humans have exclusive rights to any of these valued objects, but he may share or borrow them, provided he behaves appropriately. There is no such thing as the dog's bone. The bone is on loan to your dog; it really belongs to you and can be reclaimed at any time.

Slowly build your dogs confidence by showing him that you are not going to take things away forever. Whenever your dog is playing with his toys or chewing on a bone, periodically take it away. At first, make things easier by making an exchange. Say "Thank you," and offer a juicy chunk of chicken in exchange for the toy. The special treat also rewards him for letting you take his toy. Lavish him with praise and when he's done with the treat, give him back his toy. As the exercise proceeds, give the bribe on fewer occasions and keep the object for longer periods of time before returning it to him.

Food is a possession too. It's natural for dogs to be protective of their food and even an empty food bowl. If you were to reach for your dog's food bowl, he would probably think that you were going to take it away. Show your dog that your hand is not reaching down to take, but instead, it is reaching to give.

You can do this by hiding a special treat in your hand. Just as you extend your hand towards the food bowl, you produce the treat and drop it into the bowl. Every time your dog is eating his boring, dry kibble, walk by and drop a special treat into his bowl.

It won't be long before he realizes that it's a wonderful thing to have you approach and reach towards his bowl. He has learned that you are approaching to give, not to take.

If your dog has already exhibited aggressive behavior around his food, bones or toys, or when being handled, then it is recommended that you work with a professional trainer before doing any of the exercises that provoke your dog to growl, snap or bite.

If your dog or puppy does not exhibit any tendency to be protective or hesitant about being handled, then do these exercises as preventive maintenance to prevent problems from developing at some time in the future. With my dogs, these are life time and life long exercises. In time, the exercises themselves become interactions that are inherently rewarding.

Friendly Training

Train your dog to perform friendly and submissive behaviors such as tail wags, hand licks, shake hands and roll over. Asking your dog to sit, shake hands and then roll over to receive a prolonged tummy rub teaches him that it is fun and enjoyable to be friendly and submissive.

In many cases, simply asking your dog to obey an obedience command can prevent many problems and potentially dangerous situations. For example, instructing your dog to sit is the easiest way to keep him from jumping up. Dogs cannot sit and jump at the same time. If your dog is obediently heeling, he cannot at the same time be lunging or pulling on leash.

Spay/Neuter

Whether male or female, if your veterinarian says your dog is healthy enough to be neutered or spayed, do it without delay.

———————

For more detailed information on causes and cures for temperament and aggression problems in puppies and adult dogs, please refer to my book, *HELP! My Dog Has An Attitude.*

Chewing

Better Homes & Dogs

It's important to see things from your dog's point of view and realize that chewing is a normal dog behavior. Most dogs love to chew on stuff. For them, chewing is part of play. Whether we like it or not, that's just the way dogs are.

In addition, puppies chew to ease the pain of teething. Dogs, especially puppies, discover their environment with their paws and jaws. Investigation may lead to play and chewing continues because it is fun. Older dogs that have no previous history of destruction may suddenly start chewing because of dental problems (a trip to the vet will usually take care of this).

Holistic Approach

There are some general reasons why a dog resorts to what we consider misbehavior. When the dog is chewing, shredding, ripping and tearing things up, he doesn't think he's doing anything wrong. Most of the time he is having fun! If your dog is bored or has too much energy and nothing to do with it, he may take up a destructive pastime.

To alleviate boredom, schedule daily exercise and play sessions with your dog. A happy, well-exercised dog is more likely to sleep contentedly all day long and less likely to engage in destructive chewing. Regular walks, play sessions and training not only provide exercise but also help to improve general communication between you and your dog. This makes communicating about specific problems easier.

The chapters on barking and digging describe some games and activities you and your dog might enjoy. There are some general and obvious things you can do to make your life and your dog's life easier. Keep your shoes in the closet and keep the closet door closed. Store the trash can in a place the dog can't enter. Don't tempt and torment your dog by making it too easy for her to get into trouble. Remember, training is setting the dog up to get things right so she can be rewarded and praised.

Reward

Whether trying to prevent or cure a chewing problem, the single most important item on the agenda is rewarding your dog for chewing appropriate objects. The first order of business then is to provide your dog with chewtoys, so that she has an appropriate and acceptable outlet for this important activity.

Buy several types of chewtoys and put them all on the floor to see which ones the dog likes. Then buy a couple dozen more of each favored brand. Put a few chewtoys in every room; one on every carpet; one near every piece of furniture and one near every closet door. Put several of them outside near patio furniture, hoses, plants, etc.

Simply dumping a whole bunch of chewtoys in front of your dog is not enough. Unfortunately, your dog cannot read the labels and therefore will not know what they are for. It is important to specifically train your dog to chew these items and these items alone. Before it is fair to reprimand your dog for chewing inappropriate articles, make sure that you have made it quite clear which articles you would like her to chew. Take the time to train your dog to chew on her chewtoys.

Always be on the alert to lavish your dog with praise each and every time that she approaches and starts playing with a chewtoy without your encouragement. Don't take this for granted. In addition, you may actively help your dog to redirect chewing activities to her own toys. Put her toys on the floor and praise her each time she sniffs, licks or chews them. Make the toys more tempting by waggling them around or slowly dragging one along the floor.

Most importantly, train your dog to "find" her chewtoy. Hide it under her blanket, then tell her to go "find it." When she does so, reward her with lots of praise and affection and maybe a treat, then continue the game. The idea is to get your dog into the habit of looking for a toy even if one is not in view. Even though you may have placed several chewtoys in each room while preparing to leave, they have a tendency to disappear in no time at all.

It is usually a bad idea to use old shoes, clothing or household articles as chewtoys. Many dogs will eventually make the mistake of failing to discriminate between the shoes you give her and the shoes you don't want her to play with.

Until your dog can be trusted not to destroy your belongings, she should not be given free run of the house when you are not home or when you can't watch her. She should temporarily be confined to an area littered with appropriate toys. Since she will have no other choice of items to chew, she'll learn to play with her own toys.

Reprimand

If you catch your dog in the act of chewing a forbidden article, she should be reprimanded instantly. The reprimand should be short, sharp and instructive. Quickly shout, "OFF!" Then immediately (in a nice voice) ask her to "go find" her chewtoy. Repeat the instruction until she grabs hold of a chewtoy. She may need a little help from you in finding one. Once she has the chewtoy, praise and reward her.

This is a valuable learning experience for your dog. Within a couple of seconds, you have indicated that it is wrong for her to chew on the carpet, but that it makes you very happy to see her chew her own toys. You have communicated that it is not the chewing behavior that you find objectionable, but rather her choice of item.

Booby traps can also be used to teach your dog what she should not chew. One useful booby trap is the combination of hot sauce plus a warning cue such as a perfume. Liberally paint the hot sauce on a favorite or recently chewed item such as underneath the corners of a carpet or on a chair leg. Then put a drop of diluted perfume on the top side of the carpet or at the bottom of the chair leg. Any inexpensive perfume diluted about 1 to 100 with water will work.

You don't want your entire house to smell of perfume - you only want your dog with her keen senses to smell it. She will smell the scent, approach to investigate and eventually take a lick or chew. Usually this is a very quick lick or chew since she will be in immediate need of water! While your dog is dousing her tongue, clean off the hot sauce and spray the diluted perfume on other items of furniture or clothing.

Dogs can't read a sign that says "Danger, this is hot," but they can smell the perfume which warns them that the item is hot and they had better leave it alone. If your dog loves the taste of hot sauce, then find an appropriate, safe substitute.

Soon the habit of chewing on items other than her chewtoys will disappear and the training tools (perfume, hot sauce, etc.) will no longer be necessary.

There are products such as Bitter Apple available in pet stores that are designed to be used as taste deterrents. Also read the section on Booby Traps for more ideas on how to discourage chewing.

Fearfulness

Dog Tags of Courage

Let's put fearfulness and shyness in perspective. Many people think of these as negative traits. On the contrary, shyness is quite a normal and adaptive trait for all dogs. Shyness in itself is not a problem. It is only a problem if the dog's shyness results in other behavior problems that are often related to shyness, for example: fear-biting, submissive urination or anxiety provoked destructiveness.

The fact that a shy or fearful dog may resort to growling, snapping or biting to defend himself makes fearfulness an extremely important concern. When frightened by loud noises or sudden movements, dogs often express their fear in destructive behavior or barking.

Reward & Reprimand

In a well-meaning attempt to calm the dog's fears, many people end up inadvertently training their dog to be even more shy and fearful. When our dog cowers, hides, barks, whines, screams or snaps, our response is always the same. It is only human nature for us to feel protective and try to reassure our dog by talking soothingly, petting him or even picking him up for a big hug. These actions flagrantly reward the dog for fearful behavior.

By all means, you should have the sensitivity to realize that your dog is frightened, but you should try to ignore the shy and fearful behavior. Save your praise and reassurance for times when your dog acts with confidence. Within time, your dog will learn that hiding from visitors and barking at strangers does not make them go away and that for the most part, they are harmless anyway.

Never reprimand or punish your dog for exhibiting fear as this will make him even more fearful. But at the same time, don't ignore or reinforce aggressive behavior. Shy or fearful dogs often react defensively when approached by unfamiliar people. They may try to keep strangers away by growling, snapping or biting. These behaviors must not be ignored.

No dog should be allowed to get away with acting aggressively towards humans, no matter what the reason. The fact that your dog is shy is no excuse to condone growling, snapping or biting. Your dog must be instantly and effectively reprimanded for such behavior. Sooner or later, growling develops into biting and dogs that bite people seldom live very long.

However, since you, as the owner, are the only person your dog trusts, you are the only person who can reprimand such obnoxious behavior without destroying the dog's confidence. If it's left for strangers to reprimand your dog, it only reinforces the dog's thought that it was right to try to avoid them in the first place.

Of course, if it is ever necessary for you to reprimand aggressive tendencies in your shy dog, you should also realize that you have probably been trying to push him along too quickly. Avoid similar threatening situations until your dog has developed sufficient confidence to deal with them without resorting to biting.

The Solution

Brush up on some obedience training and teach your dog a few tricks and games. It's difficult for your dog to be frightened when he's enjoying his favorite game of fetch. It's difficult to think about whatever is frightening him when he is concentrating on a quick series of "Come here, sit, heel, sit, shake hands, lie down, roll over."

The idea is to distract your dog. You can then shower him with lots of affection and attention, but for obeying a simple command of "Sit, shake hands," instead of for acting fearful. If your dog is afraid of visitors, have them participate with you in your dog's favorite games. Laugh, giggle and show your dog by example that the visitor is not threatening and in fact, is a lot of fun.

Another method of helping your dog overcome his fear is to slowly and gradually accustom him to the situations that frighten him. For example, if your dog is afraid of particular loud noises, you can make a recording of the sounds and play it back to him while he is enjoying everyday life and activities.

Start by playing it back at such a low volume that you can barely hear it, but your dog's keen sense of hearing will. He should show no signs of fear at this volume. Gradually, over the course of weeks or months, increase the volume by tiny increments. Increase the volume so slowly that your dog will hardly notice the change. Eventually he will be used to hearing the sounds at full force. If at any time, he shows signs of fear, decrease the volume again and proceed a little more slowly.

This method will work more quickly if you incorporate fun play and training sessions into the procedure.

If your dog is shy or fearful of people, then it's up to you to socialize him. Many people try to socialize their dog too quickly, forcing him to interact with people. This usually only reinforces the dog's view that people are frightening.

On the one hand, your dog needs to be socialized as quickly as possible, but on the other hand, he should not be forced into it. If you push him to do too much too quickly, he will only become more fearful.

Socializing a dog and helping him build his confidence is a time-consuming task. Thrusting your dog into the arms of every visitor or dragging him outside to socialize with strangers can be counterproductive. Strangers should never be allowed to approach your dog and pet him. It should always be left up to your dog to make the first contact. If your dog does not want to approach, that is OK. Give him plenty of time to "hide and peek" and eventually he will come out of hiding.

Let your dog come out of his shell in his own good time. Provide him with the opportunity and be there to praise, reward and encourage his new confidence. Remember not to reward his fear.

Socializing with People

When socializing your dog with people, the goal is to give your dog the opportunity to meet people on his own terms. It is important therefore that participants are not allowed to approach your dog, look straight into his eyes, reach out for him or do anything that might make him feel pressured, fearful or forced into meeting them. Expose your dog to one person at a time and let him build confidence in several steps.

1. Invite a person to your house. When the visitor arrives, put your dog in a back room and have your guest sit quietly in a chair. Tell your guest not to speak to or even look at your dog. Then release your dog from the back room and allow him to investigate at his own speed. If he is allowed plenty of time to "hide and peek" he will soon learn that this person is no threat.

Do not actively encourage your dog to approach and do not pull him out from a hiding place. This will only slow things down and frighten him even more.

You can try to speed things up by offering a reward gradient around the visitor. Scatter pieces of food around the visitor with your dog's favorite treats closest to the visitor. With this set up, your dog can approach to get a treat and the closer he gets to the guest, the better the treat he gets. Each time he approaches he is rewarded and gains confidence, and the closer he approaches the more he is rewarded and the more confidence he gains. This method will work best when your dog is hungry.

There are no fixed rules for confidence building exercises. If your dog hides in the back room, then there is no point in setting up a food gradient in the front room. Instead, the lower end of the gradient must extend to the dog's hiding place. It may take several afternoons or evenings a week with the same person before your dog feels comfortable about approaching. However, your dog may quickly decide that fear takes a back seat to a healthy appetite and he may eagerly approach the visitor in a few minutes.

2. Once your dog will readily approach, it is time to entice him to establish first contact with the guest. If your guest simply lets an arm dangle over the side of the chair, your dog might have enough courage to steal a quick sniff. Now your encouragement and praise can be helpful. Have your visitor hold some food treats and occasionally toss one towards your dog, or just let them drop to the floor.

If things proceed smoothly, the visitor may try holding

an especially tasty treat in an outstretched hand. Once your dog will take food from your guest's hand, the guest may try holding his hand closer and closer to his own body to get your dog to approach even closer.

3. The next step is to get your dog to allow the visitor to make contact. The visitor should entice your dog to approach, then delay giving the treat for a few seconds so that your dog becomes accustomed to staying close. Next the visitor should try to reach out slowly and gently scratch your dog behind the ear before giving him the treat. If the dog balks, he does not get the food.

Your dog will quickly learn that in order to get the treat, he must first let himself be touched - first one scratch behind the ear, then two scratches and then three scratches and so on. Within time, the first fleeting contact turns into a healthy bout of gentle scratching and stroking. Now it's time to introduce a new guest to your dog starting with step one.

Socializing with Dogs

The process of socializing a dog that is shy or fearful towards other dogs is best left to other dogs. The length of time required for socialization depends very much on the dog's age. With a young puppy, it may be accomplished in a matter of weeks. All you have to do is allow your puppy to play with several other puppies and dogs a couple of times a week. With adult dogs, it is much more time consuming and may take several months or longer.

The first step towards socializing a fearful dog is to find another dog that the shy dog likes or is at least not too terrified of, and get them together on a frequent and regular basis. After a number of meetings, the dogs will establish a special relationship.

Try to find a dog that is friendly and playful. Exposing the shy or fearful dog to a young puppy usually does the trick. A shy dog is usually not overly afraid of a young puppy. The two develop a fun relationship and in just a few months, the puppy is the size of an adult dog, so now the shy dog has at least one adult sized canine friend. This does a lot to build confidence. Then try to find another pup or perhaps a gentle adult dog as an additional playmate.

Generally, it is best for the first meeting to take place on neutral territory. Arrange to meet the owner of the other dog for a long walk in an isolated area. Walk both dogs on leash. First, do not allow them to investigate each other. At the end of the walk, invite the owner and dog over to your house. The next time, the post-walk activities may take place at the other owner's house.

The longer the dogs are left together, the greater opportunity the shy dog will have to build up confidence and to begin to interact and play. Again, be careful not to reinforce shy or fearful behavior. If the dog wants to hide, that's fine. He will eventually come out of hiding. A ploy that often helps is to make a point of playing with the canine visitor.

Repeat this procedure with a couple of other dogs to further build up a canine circle of friends. Once the shy dog is confident interacting with each friend individually, it is time to invite two of them over at the same time. This really works wonders. Usually the two other dogs play and the shy dog is the outsider until he gradually learns to join in.

Now it is time for more communal walks in areas where you are likely to meet several other dogs. With the presence of his buddy or buddies (both human and canine), the shy dog will have more confidence in meeting unfamiliar dogs.

Training can be a great help when socializing a shy dog. Simply instructing your dog to heel, sit and lie down each time he encounters another dog, will help take his mind off the stress of meeting the other dog. The shy dog will feel more secure since he does not have to worry about how to act. He only has to follow your instructions.

In addition, instructing your dog to sit or lie down eases the tension during a canine encounter. A dog that is sitting or lying down is perceived as relaxed and non-threatening. Consequently, the other dog will be less likely to threaten. In turn, the shy dog will feel less threatened, so the meeting is more likely to go well. This simple procedure helps to diffuse potentially stressful situations.

The two most important rules are: do not do too much too quickly; and do not unintentionally reinforce the dog's shy behaviors. Try to find a friendly and playful adult dog or a young boisterous puppy for the shy dog to play with. Ignore any signs of fearfulness that the dog may show. If the dog becomes defensive and growls or snaps, just ignore it and leave him to back up his own threats.

Never reinforce the dog's threatening or defensive behavior by reassuring or picking him up in any attempt to calm him down. If the dogs are given enough time and are allowed to meet on several fun occasions, they will usually make friends.

If you are truly afraid that one dog will hurt the other, stop the play session and find a more suitable playmate for your dog.

Booby Traps

Outfoxing Your Dog

Booby traps operate on the principle of superstition. If your dog associates something with an unpleasant experience, he will want to avoid that particular thing in the future. Booby traps are never designed nor meant to cause physical harm, nor to torment your dog. They are used to discourage a particular activity or behavior your dog indulges in. Never set up a booby trap and leave your dog unattended.

Examples

1.   If your dog is STEALING objects such as clothing from a laundry basket, trash out of cans, food off the table or something similar, then a booby trap can effectively stop the behavior.

Take a piece of string and tie one end of it to the object your dog will try to steal. Do not use real food on counters or in trash cans. Instead, use a paper towel that has been daubed in bacon drippings or something that will attract your dog. In case the booby trap malfunctions, you don't want him to be rewarded for stealing by getting to eat the treat.

Tie the other end of the string to a shake can (an empty aluminum soda can with several pennies in it and taped shut). When the can is shaken, it makes a very loud, obnoxious noise. Set the can down, and about a foot away, place another shake can. Place a piece of cardboard on top of these two cans. Now put as many shake cans as possible on the cardboard.

When your dog tries to steal the booby trapped object, the string is pulled and down come all the cans, making a terrible racket. Your dog will think the world is crashing down around him and will probably never again approach the object that set it off. Occasionally, a booby trap needs to be set off twice before the dog learns, but usually once is enough.

2.   If your dog is JUMPING UP ON COUNTER TOPS, make a false edge to the counter by laying down a piece of cardboard so that 2 or 3 inches protrude over the edge. Weigh down the other side of the cardboard with shake cans. When the dog's paws hit what he thinks is the counter top edge, it will give way under his paws and a

dozen cans will come crashing down around him.

3. If your dog is CLAWING at certain areas (doors, windows, fences), try attaching inflated balloons to the area. When paw meets balloon, the sudden burst of air and loud noise will most likely keep your dog away from the rest of the balloons and therefore the door, fence, etc.

4. Once your dog has a healthy respect for aluminum cans and balloons, one can or balloon left on the sofa, bed or counter will keep your dog away and OFF FURNITURE.

Remember, booby traps should be just severe enough to discourage the activity but never to physically hurt or traumatize your dog. For other ideas on booby traps, refer to the sections on chewing and digging. Check your local pet store for products that are designed as deterrents and booby traps.

Housetraining
Doggie Diapers

Whether puppy or adult dog, this method of housetraining works every time:

1. Give your dog every opportunity to relieve herself in places you have chosen as her toilet area.
2. Give her zero opportunity to relieve herself anywhere else.
3. Never use reprimand for housetraining mistakes.
4. Praise and reward her every time she does her business in the right place.

The Set Up

Dogs develop habits and preferences very quickly, especially when they are young. As a result, they are usually extremely particular about where they eliminate. Every time your dog "goes" outside on grass, dirt, gravel, or concrete, she is developing a habit of going there. Likewise, every time your dog "goes" in the house, on carpet or hardwood floor, she is developing a habit of going in these places. Once the habit is established, it's time consuming and difficult to get the dog to want to go somewhere else.

Speed and ease of housetraining depend on setting up a routine which allows your dog the most opportunity to eliminate in your choice of location and the least opportunity to eliminate anywhere else. In other words - set your dog up to succeed! Three things will help you accomplish this.

FIRST: Know when your dog needs to eliminate so you can assure she is in the right place at the right time. Puppies usually eliminate every 45 minutes to one hour. Once trained, healthy adult dogs have no difficulty holding their urine for 8 to 10 hours. Dogs will usually eliminate just after waking, shortly after eating or drinking, and following vigorous exercise.

If you put your dog on a regular routine, she will adjust accordingly. You are in control of the feeding; what goes in on a regular schedule will come out on a regular schedule.

SECOND: Don't allow your dog free run of your house when you are not there to monitor her. If she eliminates in another room or behind furniture and does her business when you are not looking, then she is developing a habit of leaving puddles and piles where she chooses.

Confine your dog to a small space and paper the entire floor, or confine her to an enclosed area outside. If she does eliminate, no matter where she goes, it's OK because it'll either be outside or on papers. Your dog will be developing a habit of eliminating outside or on papers.

If you are paper training your dog, don't start reducing the area of the floor that's covered until she is accustomed to eliminating on the papers and shows a preferred location for performing her duties. Gradually reduce the area papered until you are left with only one sheet covering her preferred spot.

If she goes near, but misses the paper, you've reduced the size too quickly. She will also "miss" the paper if the paper is already soiled. Return to papering a larger area and discard wet and soiled papers immediately and replace them with fresh paper. Similarly, if you have provided a small outside area as her toilet, clean up her feces as soon as possible.

During early training some dogs are reminded of where to do their business by the scent of their own urine. If you think your dog needs this cue, then leave a very slightly damp paper on the floor and cover it with fresh dry paper. Dogs have an incredibly keen sense of smell and they will detect it.

THIRD: Crate or leash training is one of the most efficient and effective ways to control when and where your dog eliminates. Dogs do not like to soil their living quarters if given plenty of opportunity to eliminate elsewhere. Temporarily confining a dog to a small area strongly inhibits the tendency to urinate and defecate.

Since your dog is inhibited from eliminating while she is confined, she will need to go when she is released, so take her to an appropriate area straight from her confinement. Leash and crate training help teach your dog to have bladder and bowel control. Instead of going whenever she feels like it, she will learn to hold it and go at convenient, scheduled times.

Crate and leash training techniques should never be abused. Do not leave your dog unattended while she is on leash. The crate is not intended as a place to lock up your dog and forget her for extended periods of time. If the dog soils the crate because you left her confined for too long, the whole process will be meaningless. The dog has now been forced to soil her living area and consequently will be much harder to housetrain.

Whether using a leash or crate, give your dog just enough room to comfortably lie down and stretch out. Take her from room to room with you as you go about your daily household activities. Give your dog an opportunity to relieve herself about once an hour. Each time she is taken off her leash or let out of the crate, immediately take her to her designated toilet area and allow her a few minutes to do her business.

If she does not eliminate, simply put her back on leash or in her crate and try again later. However, if she does go, then immediately reward her with plenty of praise, affection, treats, a play session, a long walk and free run of the house for a couple of hours before being returned to the leash or crate (only half an hour for puppies).

Use this time to introduce your entire house, room by room to your dog. Show her that these areas are also her living area by letting her play, eat and spend time there. At night: if your adult dog has emptied herself out, she'll be able to stay over night in the crate.

For puppies, put the crate in a small room or enclosure with papers on the floor. Leave the crate door open. If she needs to go in the middle of the night, she can relieve herself on the papers and not be forced to soil her crate. Better yet, set an alarm clock and get up in the middle of the night or very early in the morning to take her out.

I like to keep the crate right next to my bed where I can hear my puppy. As soon as I hear her awaken or become restless, I get up and take her out. I have a week or so of disturbed sleep, but it's well worth it for the reward of having my puppy housetrained in as little time as possible. It isn't long before the puppy is able to hold her bladder all night long.

Reprimand

Never reprimand your dog when housetraining her, even if you catch her in the act. If you do find your dog eliminating somewhere she shouldn't - then gently pick her up or encourage her to go with you outside or to her designated toilet area. Act urgently and with concern, but never show anger or frighten your dog while she is eliminating.

If you frighten or punish her, she will learn that it is unwise to urinate or defecate in front of you. Instead, she will eliminate when left indoors alone, or more infuriatingly, she will do so when you are home but out of sight. Some dogs refuse to eliminate when taken on long walks because they are afraid to "go" in front of their owner. But immediately upon returning home, the dog eliminates in hiding behind the couch in the living room.

In housetraining, your dog never makes a mistake. If she eliminates somewhere other than where you want her to go - it's your mistake. Unless you know her bladder and bowels are empty, she shouldn't have access to areas where mistakes can happen - she shouldn't be running around your house unsupervised. If you know her bladder and bowels need to be emptied, then provide her with a place where it's OK for her to relieve herself.

Reward

The single most important aspect of any kind of training, including housetraining, is reward for appropriate behavior. Reward is the only resource you have in this case, as reprimands do not work and only make housetraining more time consuming and difficult. Dogs, cats, and even humans learn much more quickly when taught by reward methods rather than punishment.

All the aspects of housetraining discussed so far are to ensure that your dog gets it right. If she gets it right, that means you can reward and praise her. Whenever your dog eliminates in an appropriate area, you should make it quite clear that she has done a most wonderful and glorious thing!

Don't limit your reward to verbal praise. Anything the dog enjoys can be used as a reward. A walk is one of the best rewards for a dog once she has eliminated. Most of us take our dogs for walks to give them a chance to eliminate. All too often, the walk comes to an abrupt end once the dog "goes." We feel our mission has been accomplished so it's time to return home.

Most dogs catch on quickly and will delay eliminating just to extend the walk. They learn that once emptied out, they are immediately whisked back home. But if you put off the walk until your dog has eliminated, she will learn the basics of housetraining in no time at all.

The reward of a walk is worth more than a million verbal praises.

Urine Marking

Squatter's Rights

A dog may be perfectly housetrained yet still lift his leg to urine mark in your house. Females will urine mark too. Urinating and marking are two different functions. Urinating is a physiological process of eliminating waste. Urine marking is a territorial, social and sexual behavior.

While it is inappropriate to reprimand your dog during housetraining, it is definitely appropriate to use reprimand when curing a urine marking problem. Neutering your dog will often help prevent or stop urine marking.

As with all behavior problems, it is essential to first show and teach your dog what you want him to do. It's OK for him to mark outside, so let's tell him. Praise and reward him profusely every time he urine marks outside. When he is convinced that you approve of his marking outside, then you can tell him that marking inside is not allowed.

When treating any behavior problem, it's a good idea to either review some basic obedience training with your dog or enroll him in an obedience class. This will not in and of itself get rid of the problem, but it does help reinforce the line of communication and respect between the two of you.

Nothing will entice a male dog to urinate more than the smell or presence of another dog's urine. Using cotton balls, soak up some urine from another dog. Tack a couple of the urine-soaked cotton balls to a post outside and let your dog discover them. As soon as he sniffs and squirts, praise and reward him.

Now, it's time to teach him not to mark inside. Find a safe location indoors and tack one of the cotton balls there. Watch your dog very closely. As soon as he begins to sniff and position himself to lift his leg (but before he actually urinates), scream "NO! BAD DOG! GO OUTSIDE, OUTSIDE, OUTSIDE!" and chase him outdoors.

As soon as he gets outside, he'll find the post where you've previously tacked six or seven cotton balls. When he urinates on them, praise him profusely. In just a few seconds, he's learned that trying to mark indoors makes you angry but marking outdoors makes you very happy and he gets rewarded for it. Before trying this exercise, be sure your dog knows what the word "outside" means.

The key to this method is timing. If there is any delay whatsoever in the timing of the praise or reprimand, the procedure in meaningless. Never show your dog his mistake and scold him. In order for this procedure to work, you must catch your dog in the act of urine marking.

Submissive & Excitement Urination
Puddle Patrol

It's normal for dogs to urinate when they become excited or when they want to demonstrate submission. Even a dog that is otherwise housetrained may leave dribbles and puddles of urine at your feet and on the floor when greeting you.

SUBMISSIVE URINATION is the ultimate show of respect and deference for higher rank. Dogs that urinate submissively are insecure and usually have not been shown that there are more acceptable ways to show respect, such as paw raising (shake hands) or hand licking (give a kiss).

Other dogs submissively urinate because they feel the need to constantly apologize. This state is often caused by excessive or delayed punishment which frightens and confuses the dog without teaching her how to make amends. The dog resorts to the only way she knows to show respect and fear, by urinating.

When your dog urinates in this manner, it is best to just ignore her. If you try to reassure her, she will think you are praising her for urinating and will urinate even more. If you scold her, she will feel an even greater need to apologize by urinating.

Treatment must be directed towards building your dog's confidence and showing her other ways to demonstrate respect. The quickest way to accomplish this is by teaching your dog a few basic obedience exercises.

A dog that can earn praise by obeying a simple routine of "Come here, sit, shake hands," will soon develop self esteem and confidence. A confident dog who can say, "Hello, Boss" by sitting and shaking hands does not feel the need to urinate at her owner's feet.

EXCITEMENT URINATION usually occurs in puppies and is caused by lack of bladder control. The dog is not aware that he is urinating, and any punishment will only confuse him. Since he does not know why you are angry, the excitement urination will quickly become submissive urination in an attempt to appease you. As your puppy matures and develops bladder control, the problem will usually disappear. However, in the mean time, it is probably a good idea to do something to help keep your puppy dry.

The best treatment for excitement urination is to prevent your dog from becoming overly excited in the first place. You can do this by exposing your dog to the stimulus that excites him, over and over until it no longer excites him. Most likely, your dog gets excited and wets when you return home. If so, simply ignore him for about 10 minutes. Don't even look at him.

Then leave again for a few minutes, return and ignore, leave, return and ignore. Keep doing this until you can see that your dog is not only unexcited, but is actually getting bored with the whole thing. If your dog gets overly excited when visitors arrive, have them do this too. When your dog has calmed down and is no longer excited when you come in, then very quietly and gently say hello. If any signs of excitement appear, quickly exit and repeat the coming-and-going routine. A rapid sequence of heel-sits will capture your dog's attention and channel his excitement to the game of heeling and sitting.

As with submissive urinating, remember to also ignore excitement urination and never scold or get angry at your dog when either of these occur.

Confinement

Rover's Romper Room

Confinement is no different than putting a baby in a play pen. When mom is cooking dinner in the kitchen and can't watch the baby, she puts her in a playpen so she stays out of trouble and doesn't get hurt.

She doesn't expect the baby to know that the stove is hot or that the stairs are dangerous. We don't expect babies to know what's valuable. But for some reason, we often expect our dogs to know these things. We want them to read our minds and magically know what they should or shouldn't do. Or we feel that if we've told them a few times, they should remember perfectly every time.

The play pen is not a jail. When kids get used to it, they learn to entertain themselves and enjoy their play pen. That's why they're called play pens. When you confine your dog, you should have the same attitude. This is a special place for your dog. You should consider it the dog's playroom.

Make the room a pleasant and fun place to be. Introduce it slowly and gradually; spend time there with your dog until he feels confident in his own special haven. Don't just toss him in and walk away. Give him things to do in there; make it his favorite place.

Start out by confining him for very short periods of time - a few minutes at the most. Gradually increase the time until you can leave him for several hours. If done correctly, dogs actually love confinement. It gives them a place of security and comfort.

Your dog isn't going to be confined forever - just until he can be trusted to have full run of the house. Confinement is prevention. For example: your dog will be prevented from developing a taste for and habit of chewing the couch if the couch is not in his playroom.

Confinement also helps your dog develop good habits. If the only available objects to chew on are his chewtoys, then he will develop a habit of chewing them simply because there is nothing else there to chew.

Temporary confinement can be useful for several reasons:

1. There is no need to have your home and property destroyed while you are trying to teach your dog good manners. If your dog is confined, your belongings are safe.

2. An untrained dog, running loose in the house, can hurt himself by chewing electrical cords, eating poisonous plants, getting into hazardous chemicals, etc.

3. Confinement is a useful tool in shaping your dog's behavior and habits. You can use confinement to prevent bad habits from forming and as a method of establishing good habits.

Separation Anxiety Or Separation Fun

How Do You Spell Relief

Many dogs whine, bark, cry, scratch at the door or destroy your home and yard when left alone. We often unintentionally train our dogs to behave this way because whenever they throw this kind of tantrum when we leave, we quickly come back to reassure them, give them attention or even a bone or biscuit. If you do this, your dog will soon learn that she can control you with emotional blackmail.

Long, drawn-out farewells can excite your dog and make the isolation more obvious when you're gone. Just when she gets all worked up and ready to play, suddenly you disappear. With all this energy, your dog will either try her best to get you to come back or she will have to vent her energy in some other way. Since she can't build model airplanes or invite her friends over for a cup of tea, she does doggy things - like chew, dig and bark.

We often think our dog is destructive because she is angry that we left her, but she's really just trying to have some fun since there is nothing else to do. She may be relieved to be able to do those things she normally can't do when you're home. She may be thinking, "Thank goodness the owner is finally leaving! Now I can chase the cat, dig up the tomatoes, get in the trash, and bark at the neighbors. They never let me do those things when they're home."

Some dogs are stressed, nervous and insecure when they are left alone. They express this nervous energy in typical dog fashion - chewing, digging, barking and housesoiling.

Dogs need to feel happy, secure, and comfortable when you're away. It's important to give them things to do while you're gone. Provide them with lots of toys or a digging pit in the yard. Often another companion pet can help alleviate the boredom.

When you are home, set aside scheduled time periods to give your dog undivided attention, play and exercise. A happy, well-exercised dog will usually sleep contentedly during the day while you are gone. Be sure that one of the scheduled play sessions occurs before you must leave for the day. Give your dog a chance to settle down before you leave and don't make a big deal of your departure - just leave without any emotion or commotion.

If your dog is not used to being left alone or already has panic attacks when you leave, then gradually accustom her to your leaving. Practice leaving and returning several times a day until she gets used to your departures and realizes that you are not abandoning her forever. Gradually leave for longer and longer periods of time, but start out by leaving for just 5 minutes and returning again.

Breaking
Bad Habits
Dog Day Afternoons

Dogs often go berserk and become uncontrollable when specific things happen - when someone comes to the door, when you come home, when children walk by the fence, when a cat or dog passes by your home, yard or even the car. Dogs will bark, jump, lunge, madly dash around, growl and even urinate when excited.

Many times this behavior was accidentally taught to your dog. When he jumped up, he was rewarded with attention. When he barked or acted territorial, you might have said something like, "Oh Rover, there's nothing to get excited about, now you settle down and be a good boy." Your dog didn't understand your words, but he did know that he was getting positive and rewarding attention, so he thought he must have been doing the right thing. If you shout and get excited, he might think you're encouraging him and joining in on the excitement and barking.

The first step in stopping this type of behavior is to stop rewarding it. The next step is to isolate whatever it is that sets your dog off and repeat it over and over again until he is bored half to death with it. For example: If your dog goes bonkers every time the neighbor's son walks by the fence, then ask your neighbor's son if he wants to earn a few dollars by spending a Saturday morning helping you train your dog. All he has to do is keep walking by your fence over and over.

At first, Rover will charge and bark at the fence as usual and you may think he'll never stop. After your neighbor's son has passed by the fence 10 or 20 times, or as many as 100 times, Rover will eventually lose interest. If your dog looks up at all, he'll probably just think, "Oh, you again." Continue exposing your dog to the exciting stimulus repeatedly until he becomes blase and thinks, "Ho hum."

As your dog begins to get bored with the stimulus, you can then get his attention to train him to respond differently. For example: If your dog goes nuts every time the doorbell rings, have someone sit outside your door and ring the bell every 30 seconds. During this time, you can devote all your attention to your dog and train him to bark several times then go to his basket and lie down. In the past, every time the doorbell rang, your attention had to go to the visitor. You didn't have time at that moment to train your dog, so he got away with all kinds of undesirable behavior.

Keep in mind how many weeks, months or years your dog has been misbehaving and don't expect the problem to disappear in an hour. You must devote some time and patience to this. Give your dog lots of opportunity and practice at behaving appropriately. Don't forget to reward and praise his good behavior - he'll learn much more quickly.

Printed in Great Britain
by Amazon.co.uk, Ltd.,
Marston Gate.